I0867586

ghost smoke

ghost smoke

JONATHAN WEINERT

H. L. HIX

BRIDWELL PRESS
Southern Methodist University, Dallas, Texas

Bridwell Press is the professional publishing arm of Bridwell Library
(SMU Libraries and Perkins School of Theology).
Southern Methodist University

SMU Libraries SMU Perkins School of Theology

Copyright © 2026 Jonathan Weinert and H. L. Hix
All rights reserved.

Series Editor: David Caplan
Design: Alicia Beebe

Printed in the United States of America

ISBN: 978-1-957946-53-5 (hardcover)
ISBN: 978-1-957946-52-8 (paperback)
ISBN: 978-1-957946-51-1 (ebook)

Cover image: Barbara Bosworth , *Moonlight in the backyard,* © 2015

SMU Project Poëtica

CONTENTS

ADVANCE PRAISE

Writing together, in one voice, the dazzlingly inventive Jonathan Weinert and H. L. Hix are more than a duet; the two poet-friends (individually sublime writers) are a blend, like a luxurious tweed, or a spirited whiskey, or a vigorous hybrid tree. With *Ghost Smoke* we're in their poetry laboratory, where they mix the everyday with searching philosophy. Unafraid to explore feelings, think-y, but gossipy and loving, Weinert and Hix are relaxed aerialists, one flying, the other catching, yet both in the air at once. *Ghost Smoke* is a beautiful and brilliant book.

—**Molly Peacock**, *author of A Friend Sails in on a Poem*

What is "the music of hinges"? Does it take its place between two authors who become, in part, the authors of each other? Or between readers and whatever readers start reading? Does it stop when we stop? Does it pull out all the stops? What are its "gauzy residuals," and might they be mirrors, as well as smoky windows? How do its geographically drifting afterimages come to seem to see us? These two poets borrow from one another so intensely that they become a third, no, a fourth, no, a perfect fifth: their language, in broken-up semi-paragraphs of meteorological genealogy (like Forrest Gander's geologies), in iterative musings, in its "water cortège," becomes leaves of meditation as various as the botanies that it also observes, "heart-shaped and serrate," "an envelope inside a fire," a yearning, a "mishap on Mrs. Foote's spinet" become a sharable epiphany. Spend time with this whole book. Get lost in it. You'll find your way into the clouds. Or your way home.

—**Stephanie Burt**, *author of We Are Mermaids*

The image of two relay runners during the precarious baton handoff came to me, reading *Ghost Smoke*. No individual effort matters if this handoff fails. Hence, there is tension which is always good for poetry—and especially in this book. I felt the stride-by-stride calibration, an intense listening, a synchronization, language touched by both, shuttled between. Then some wildness borne of this shuttling would take off and return again to the tense exchange. What these generous two-as-one poets make is a book as curriculum: an encircling, coming around again and again, like circling Jericho to bring the faulty walls of individuation down. I'm now thinking, we are all collaborating all the time, as we write and read—and so I thank Hix and Weinert for this project to teach us how to recalibrate authorship back to human which is never one.

—**Jill Magi**, *author of My Penelope*

∴

"There is no poem of one's own," write Hix-Weinert or Weinert-Hix, this writing-reading phenomenon that is no longer two and is much more than one. A collaboration that spans twenty years of an intimacy born and buoyed by writing, *Ghost Smoke* is a voice, a "single sounding-through" drawing us directly into its expansive, and gorgeous, soundscape. Their deep phenomenological attunement to the particulars of land, weather, and time—"a cottonwood leaf tracked in wet and flat but now curled dry," "Light snow overnight omened the afternoon eclipse"—calls us too to attend. "You should see the squirrels and sparrows here / moonscaping with their dustbaths," they say. I am convinced by the delicate and pulsing beauty of this writing that we can only hear "the nameless that exceeds us" together.

—**Julie Carr,** *author of The Garden and, with Lisa Olstein, Climate*

Breakout Fires

An Introduction

THE WORD "COLLABORATION" can designate a process or the outcome of a process. Both senses apply to *Ghost Smoke*. We engaged in collaboration, and you have in your hands our collaboration. The collaboration we engaged in mattered to us, and we hope that the collaboration you hold may matter to you. So, without pretending that it accounts for the collaboration you hold, we begin with a brief account of the collaboration we engaged in.

Ghost Smoke has a history.

For all its *feeling* spontaneous to us when it started, in fact this composition has a history. The two of us live far apart and have met face-to-face only two or three times, but we have been in communication for a good two decades now. We have read one another's work, we have corresponded, one of us has interviewed the other, and so on.

Our correspondence has happened largely in hard-copy postal form. We both value the texture of written communication, its deliberate pace, and how the materiality of the paper and the script, with its blemishes and errors and crossings-out, brings the other into *presence* in a way that electronic communication cannot. Very occasionally within our postal correspondence one of us would write the other a letter-poem, but starting in the autumn of 2023 we fell into a little flurry of letter-poems that lasted the better part of a year.

When we began exchanging these letter-poems, we had no inkling of where the exchange would lead. We had no sense that it would, or should, lead anywhere. We wrote simply for the pleasure of being in conversation with one another over time and distance. In other words, we recognized the exchange as something we valued in itself, before we conceived of composing, by way of another exchange, this poem-book that draws on our initial exchange.

Our communication with one another was ghost smoke before it was *Ghost Smoke*.

***Ghost Smoke* employed a method.**

Once we began to imagine that we might be able to make from our various exchanges over the years something different, we started thinking differently about the content of those exchanges. What if we treated those exchanges not as an archive, a collection of letters, poems, interviews, reviews, and so on, but as a resource, raw material for something entirely new?

Without having a definite notion what this "something entirely new" would be or what shape it might take, and even without explicitly *deciding* to do something new or ever quite "saying out loud" that we *were* doing something new, we started taking turns sampling the letter-poems we had sent, extracting passages, revising and recontextualizing them. We rewrote them as we went along so that what was spoken by one of us to the other might now be spoken by the other to the one, and what was written in answer to one thing now might answer another. In other words, A sent B material A had sent B in a different form and context, and also sent B material that B had previously written to A, but sent it as if A were writing it to B. And vice versa. A first-B-written-to-A moment might become a now-A-written-to-B moment or a B-rewritten-to-A-in-a-new-context moment, and the other way around.

In short, we experimented. Our method was experimental in the strict sense of the term: attempting something without knowing in advance whether the attempt would succeed or fail, or what the outcome would be. As in: "What if we mixed this here ammonium nitrate fertilizer with that there fuel oil?" Or: "What if we got Aubrey and Cameron to go on a blind date?"

"Ghost Smoke" *emerged* out of our first fumbling attempts to make something coherent, or at least interesting, out of the material we had to hand. We wanted exchange, call and response, to serve as an organizing principle, but we also wanted not merely to replicate things others had done in *their* collaborations. We knew a number of exchanges between contemporaries we admire: Leslie Scalapino and Lyn Hejinian together writing their books *Sight* and *Hearing*, Forrest Gander and John Kinsella assembling their *Redstart*, Natalie Diaz and Ada Limón sending their letter-poems to one another. Such a list could continue for a good long while, maybe, but it couldn't offer up any kin closer than cousins. We wanted *alternation*, but we also wanted *convergence*, such that the reader wouldn't necessarily know which one of us wrote which bits, such that even we ourselves might lose track. (We sometimes did.)

We were guided at every moment by precedents. Ancient Greek tragedy often deploys *stichomythia*, a form of dialogue in which two characters converse in alternating lines. The patterning of the exchange, its regularity and strictness and concision, releases the language from the lives of the characters into a life of its own, a meaning not contained in any one line, but arising from the patterning of lines, not in their alternation only, but in the convergence.

The Japanese verse form renku provides another formal antecedent, requiring as it does collaboration, one voice calling and the other responding, then caller and responder shifting and exchanging roles. Renku's way of linking two voices together can produce a surprising third, the voice of an other with a history and a way of seeing neither the caller's nor the responder's own. For this composition, as in renku, the links reach both across the shuttle of words and beyond them.

If our linking and shifting gave life to a new voice, then that voice needed to be *embodied*, in a structure or a form. At one point one of us suggested employing a variation on the crown of sonnets, a form capacious enough to hold all of the material we had gathered, and one that offers its own additional method of linking.

A crown of sonnets is a sequence of fourteen sonnets, in which the last line of the first sonnet becomes the first line of the second sonnet, the last line of the second becomes the first line of the third, and so on throughout. A *royal* crown adds a mastersonnet at the end: a fifteenth sonnet consisting of all of the sonnets' first lines or last lines, in order of appearance. Our mastersonnet uses all of the last lines, to achieve a kind of closure. We imposed a constraint on ourselves, toward which and by which we found ourselves unconstrained.

As for the sonnets themselves, we took many liberties. We used the Petrarchan version of the sonnet as a template (two stanzas of four lines followed by two stanzas of three lines) rather than the Shakespearean version (three stanzas of four lines followed by a couplet). We did away with the traditional rhyme scheme, and even with the traditional notion of the line. Each "line" in "Ghost Smoke" consists of a brief series of phrases or sentences, punctuated only by small gray boxes (▪). We made no rules regarding the length of these sections, but each section receives its own page. Each section also receives an introductory epigraph from a writer one of us admires. The result is a poem of two hundred and ten short sections, accompanied by sixty epigraphs. These epigraphs form a sort of community that accompanies the poem on its way, first by creating a cento (a work collaged from passages of other works), the section "Still-in-the-Sky Ice Crystals," and then by motivating the "(each. other.)" section, a kind of breviary of blessings returned for blessings received.

Once we hit on the principle of alternation and the overarching structure, we quickly established a rhythm in which we each added three sections to the poem every day, exchanging the growing typescript by email, until the whole was complete. In practice, we each added, and in some cases altered or rewrote, snippets of both our own material and each other's, blurring the distinctions between them.

Ghost Smoke posed questions.

Some years ago, A, or was it B, said something to B, or was it A, about the possibility of finding a language that could allow people to become more "porous" to one another. B, or maybe A, it hardly matters which, wasn't certain what all the implications were, but found the idea intriguing. B (or A) went on to speculate that it might even be possible to "become" one another in the conversation, whatever that might mean. This book exists in furtherance of that speculation.

The process of composition—the collaboration we engaged in—posed a series of ongoing questions for us. Ongoing, as in: They *remain* questions for us. We experience them as questions that do not admit of definitive, once-and-for-all answers, but insistently retain their interrogative force and thus their incitement to reflection: less like "Which is the highest peak in the Andes?" and more like "What is the good for humans?" One of our hopes for the collaboration you hold is not that it be answer-giving but that it be reflection-inciting.

The collaboration we engaged in posed to us such questions as the following. We hope that the collaboration you hold invites questions of your own.

- What if *presence* were a verb?
- What if intimacy were less a matter of physical adjacency and more a matter of metaphysical propinquity?
- What would it mean if two people shared each other's language—not only quoting each other, but using each other's language interchangeably?
- Is it possible to effect the switch from answering to a name, as in turning one's head when one hears it spoken, to answering to a name, as in holding oneself accountable to its implications?
- Does becoming more porous to another entail becoming more transparent to oneself? (*Can* becoming more porous to another result in becoming more transparent to oneself?)
- Can one arrive at meaning not by trying, but by giving up?
- What if we assume (what if we *acknowledge*) that the language knows more than we do?
- Can two people relate to one another in a way that relates them both to the nameless that exceeds them?
- Can we become each other's ghosts, open to and inhabited by one another? What happens to us, and what happens between us, if we do?

Ghost Smoke changed us.

It is easier to say how this composition happened between us than to say why it mattered to us—as perhaps is true of anything that matters, for anyone to whom it matters.

At first, it mattered *that* we were talking to each other. Then it mattered *how* we were talking to each other. Finally, it mattered *what* we said to each other.

A gift of friendship: One friend can say to the other what otherwise would be spoken into the void. A gift of acceptance: One friend can leave unsaid to the other what saying would void. A gift of postal correspondence: In it the tempo of communion replaces the tempo of commerce.

One thing this account is an account of: unaccountable happiness. At one point, one of us observed to the other that a piece B had just added from A came from a poem A had composed entirely of phrases B had spoken when A had interviewed B years ago. "So this language has resonated between us several times," A noted, adding "This makes me unaccountably happy." Of course it made B unaccountably happy, too.

The English word *person* derives from the Latin *personare*, to sound through, compounded from the prefix *per-*, meaning through, and the verb *sonare*, meaning to sound or utter—created by reference to the masks through which performers spoke or sang in Greek and Roman drama. The person is neither the mask itself nor the body behind it, but the speaking through it. In the sense that collaboration made our words a single sounding-through, it made us one person.

We found the imposition of shape *onto* material also a discovery of shape *within* material. We find them hard to distinguish, impossible to separate: the urge for shape, for the shaped, and for the shaping. We found pleasure in finding, for the duration of the exchange and in the process of the exchange, a way not to distinguish ourselves from one another. We found in the form a form of finding out.

One of the mysteries at which we wonder, from within it: We feel most ourselves when most one another, most individual when most merged, most attuned to the One when alert to the other.

Another mystery: listening to another's language can be a way to listen for oneself.

And another: finding a person parallel to oneself helps one be a parallel person *for* oneself. Making oneself another's ghost can feel like discovering that one was that other's ghost already.

***Ghost Smoke* belongs to you.**

Ghost smoke nods to nothing because ghost smoke is next to nothing. From the clamorous world of countless voices all speaking at once, we retreat into one voice at a time. We thank you for sitting with us in this quiet corner.

In a world of public discourse dominated by talking over others, we take refuge in listening to one another. May you find moments of sanctuary through listening in on this particular listening-to.

Still-in-the-Sky Ice Crystals

The poem begins in silence.
You may confidently / serve me snow:
I looked into his eyes / which were far larger than mine
I ascribe to you combustive ozone & witness

There was never this hour, nor this light, nor this person that's me.
Damn. braces: Bless relaxes.
My body and this field have become a single horizon,
oh, what shall I say, how is the truth to be said?

What I'm waiting for: someone to shout instructions from the sky
proud restraining purity / Restores
Not till dawn becomes a volunteer / Will we know how it was inside this world;
language is a medium for experiencing experience.

My eyes fill with a seeing not their own.
what we have heard in some other life.
we create life worlds around these wants.
We're dated within histories of make / in order to be made whole;

the imaginary joins the real in a space that contains its own secret
Slow moving and black lines go ceaselessly over the earth,
looking out / at moonstruck trees
the self that you were born with turns into / The self that you created,

like a campfire glimpsed in the distance,
Want-hands huming / upwards from my inwards
A first unfallen / church it might have been.
we have no other interior than the world.

+

More than bones, ghost- / thin skin, I'm here,
it is this visionary reality we need,
demented by brevity, / driven askew, evaporating.
But generalized magnificences cannot replace the nettle of the ravines

+

We must go beyond beyond to a place where we have never been the center,
between *always* and *to be*, / The music of hinges,
happiness and love, happiness or love.
Then there we are / side by side, looking out at the branches,

+

nothing of north / unknown, as the dark / comes earlier.
When I speak now I discern a new frequency / and different others listen.
being addressed constitutes us as subjects from the very beginning.
Don't you know this is a poem about longing?

+

my self-consciousness is not only suspended, but temporarily abolished
the farthest outpost of solitude nothing can touch,
Your mind / like a pilot light inside your sleep,
none / of the words I hold would salve and lily

+

to be in a landscape / where purity isn't possible
Concentrations of impurity serially interrupt and entangle one another.
treetops so distant / they register at first as smoke.
between oneself and the thing all the vertical, the refusal, of height.

+

Your whole age sits between what you hear / and what you write
or call / into a well where someone has fallen in.
The fragment as spoken by the one lost His heart singing in its dish
She broods on clouds, / hears voices in wind.

+

the negative where all identity is lost,
And then there was the nothing that was something else,
true existence is in the Abyss. *Yes*, trusted to night and silence.
I want everyone here to survive what is coming.

+

clouds parting, // low rumble of thunder, then / light
In other words, there is no poem of one's own,
The seamless transfer of two people / humming
remarks on the barely perceptible disappearances from our world

+

Things look different when we do not / defend ourselves from them.
together, / without meaning to, without meaning anything, / we sang
And the memory of the dust vanished immediately.
We need not fear these   silences, —

Ghost Smoke

The poem begins in silence.

My echo ▪ I'm beside myself ▪ a wind blows through me like the
wind that passes through the bankrupt sheep farm barn on Crescent
Street ▪ its paneless sills ▪ its silo full of silence

▪ ▪ ▪

Eye-level offers generous gifts but so does looking down ▪
the throw rug keeps a quiet chronicle ▪ a cottonwood leaf tracked
in wet and flat but now curled dry ▪ one thread frayed from the sleeve
of the ratty sweatshirt I pick at absentmindedly ▪
fragile legacy ▪ gauzy residuals

▪ ▪ ▪

The cold fell and the snow fell ▪ limning chimney pipes and throwing
shawls over all the finches' nests and groundhog warren holes ▪ I
stayed all day in my Psycho Bunny PJs ▪ my calf-length belted scotch
plaid robe ▪ The snowlight blued itself inside like memory ▪ myself
remembering the light in which I see myself myself remembering

▪ ▪ ▪

Light snow overnight omened the afternoon eclipse ▪ *Any* snow and
the pass ten miles east turns treacherous ▪ so they're quick to close
the interstate ▪ I felt the hush inside before I stepped outside to hear
it ▪ and only hours later felt the eclipse before I stepped outside
to see it

▪
▪

You may confidently / serve me snow:

Darken doesn't capture what the eclipse did to the sky ▪ We don't have the word we need for when alignment ▪ instead of *replacing* light by deflection *reasserts* it ▪ as particle and wave ▪ and spirit

▪ ▪ ▪

The snow fell down the empty chimney mouth ▪ the fire fingers reached ▪ and in the heart-like secret space inside the chimney's dark ▪ a hot rain formed and fell

▪ ▪ ▪

No more need to settle where the silver of reflected light ▪ sieved through a sheer of still-in-the-sky ice crystals ▪ separates from the silver glinting off ice crystals glittering already-on-the-ground powder ▪ than need to distinguish where I can no longer go ▪ from where I could never

▪ ▪ ▪

By which I mean on the day of the eclipse ▪ I stepped out into the beaten silver false midafternoon dusk ▪ The world cinema screen came down and gathered everything into it ▪ flat and pewter-smeared ▪ What I mean is where else merge with something larger than myself?

▪

▪

I looked into his eyes / which were far larger than mine

What I mean is the shadow of a crow moving too quickly to see the
crow ▪ What I mean is a cloud the exact shape of the dogwood
it rides above ▪ What I mean is five kinds of woodpecker ▪
seven kinds of sparrow

▪ ▪ ▪

What I mean is I don't *feel* old ▪ but I'm colder now than the
thermostat says I should be ▪ By *now* I mean both *at this moment* and
these days ▪ and by *I'm colder* I describe both body and soul

▪ ▪ ▪

I think now that this poem should be a whisper ▪ a thing said almost
inaudibly into one another's ears ▪ a thing that must be said but
distantly ▪ like ghost smoke rolling across a long dim field

▪
▪

I ascribe to you combustive ozone & witness

No word names the ghostliness that gives ghost smoke the ghostliness
it gives ▪ I trust how you say you say nothing ▪ I hear the nothing
you don't say in the nothing you do ▪ It's afternoon here all morning
and it's evening all afternoon ▪ Send word because there is between
us ▪ that for which there are no words

▪ ▪ ▪

Send word because the result is something peripheral ▪ some echo or
resonance or after-image ▪ because putting stuff together might be
the task ▪ it slows down the speed at which we receive the words

▪ ▪ ▪

Send word to eyedropper-feed our birdmouth urge ▪ to listen
to rain-glossolalic downspouts and look at rain-lensed driveway
divots ▪ our urge to watch for echoes and listen for reflections ▪ of
the Unmeasured Measurer

+

There was never this hour, nor this light, nor this person that's me.

Send word to eyedropper-feed our birdmouth urge ▪
to listen to rain-glossolalic downspouts and look at rain-lensed
driveway divots ▪ our urge to watch for echoes and listen for
reflections ▪ of the Unmeasured Measurer

▪ ▪ ▪

Large volumes of air move through the limbs of the five-
trunked pine ▪ while beyond the pine white oaks inscribe
what look like lightning glyphs against the sky ▪ each one
similardifferent ▪ stripped but not simple ▪ suggesting an
excessive minimalism ▪ like late-career Morton Feldman

▪ ▪ ▪

Maybe where I can no longer go always was where I could never
▪ no longer where the kite string led my eye ▪ or where loneliness
led my fingertips ▪ never where Dawn Upshaw's voice drifts ▪ after
that last long lento of Górecki's Third

▪ ▪ ▪

I'm not sure of anything but the construction of me in me ▪ To know
the self as construction means you can disappear into anything ▪
but is that true ▪ I'm writing it to try it on

▪

▪

Damn. braces: Bless relaxes.

I've been more windsock than motorbike ▪ in love with stillness and
the spaces between things ▪ in love with the silence between the
paint and the wall ▪ in love with doing nothing

▪ ▪ ▪

I doubt it's steppings out of one's body that bring on breakings into
blossom ▪ and I mistrust *Suddenly I realize* ▪ but I do treasure
blessings those receivings and givings ▪ that defy selling and
buying ▪ getting and spending

▪ ▪ ▪

I'm doing nothing as a protest ▪ nothing as resistance ▪ breathing
the air between the figures of supposed value ▪ which is all the air we
have ▪ the nothing between the figures ▪ which is the source and
the end of all value

▪ ▪ ▪

I would be the prickle of invisible ice crystals suspended in the air
before a snow ▪ I would be the symmetry of the f-holes in the belly
of a cello ▪ the texture of the surface of an old dog's paw pads ▪
the vigilance of the bubble in a level

▪
▪

My body and this field have become a single horizon,

Bathed in an afterlight I see the sugar maples in early leaf against the
background of their own disappearance ▪ It's hard not to think of
what I see as air in transition ▪ or less than air ▪ a Canada goose
calling into the coming dark

▪ ▪ ▪

It's hard not to think of what I see as a hollow bronze horse ▪
acquiescing to the centuries ▪ to the salt ▪ and the sea floor ▪
a form outlosting the wax lost voluming it into attitude

▪ ▪ ▪

People say *mm*-hm ▪ people say *I'm on my way* ▪ people say
but yeah we're good ▪ people say *it went pretty smooth* ▪
people say *this is what I would buy right here* ▪ people say *every day*
except for Sunday

▪
▪

oh, what shall I say, how is the truth to be said?

People say *don't get your hopes up* and *don't go there* ▪ people say *I'll try one more time but then I give up* ▪ people say *thanks for sharing* ▪ people say *ka-ching* and *difference-maker* and *you got yourself a deal*

▪ ▪ ▪

I *do* hear what I *would* hear if it were raining ▪ I listen *as if* for echoes and look *as if* for reflections ▪ because the listening not the hearing is the point ▪ the looking not the seeing ▪ Maybe not in the same way but the aspen and I both are waiting for the rain

▪ ▪ ▪

I remember the last time I felt this way ▪ I brought metal in a box ▪ a half head of deer ▪ cloven ▪ clovered ▪ clove of bone ▪ that savory radius ▪ My cells fill with liquids not their own

+

What I'm waiting for: someone to shout instructions from the sky

I remember the last time I felt this way ▪ I brought metal in a
box ▪ a half head of deer ▪ cloven ▪ clovered ▪ clove of
bone ▪ that savory radius ▪ My cells fill with liquids not their own

▪ ▪ ▪

I backfill what feeling calls for but memory doesn't supply ▪ for
example the alphabet scroll ▪ (Aa Bb Cc Dd...) ▪ that must have
been scotch-taped to beige-painted cinder block ▪ to cap the
blackboard in my kindergarten classroom

▪ ▪ ▪

I write *around* what I can't write *through* ▪ as starlight skirts around
the planet's sphere of influence and so on into space ▪ That first
moment of separation ▪ I can't remember it ▪ but I *feel* it's
there ▪ exerting force

▪ ▪ ▪

The tree that fell into the yard took down a whole lilac ▪ plus a goodly
length of fence ▪ but just missed the house ▪ I shoveled at the
stump for a day or two before my neighbor Mike ▪ a big guy retired
from rail repair for Union Pacific and now the voluntary super on the
block ▪ wrapped a chain around the rootball and pulled it out with his
big-ass diesel pickup

▪
▪

proud restraining purity / Restores

To put it another way ▪ why is there something rather than
nothing ▪ and how can the soul attain purity if it's manifest ▪ and
how can the soul be reabsorbed into perfection once it's fallen away ▪ as
the pure would have to be inaccessible ▪ to safeguard its purity

▪ ▪ ▪

I see why they saw the sky as a colander ▪ stars as
perforations ▪ those perorating ancients ▪ Looks to me too
like a Great Light shines through it ▪ a Light that we see through it
to ▪ *We see through it too* they protest ▪ all those nightjars flying
with the ricks and light-winged dryads of the trees ▪ I know there's no
Light Beyond ▪ but seeing through to it still feels urgent

▪ ▪ ▪

It rained four inches overnight ▪ but by the time the Shop-Vac
arrived the cellar floor was dry ▪ The temps fell into the arctic all that
following week ▪ and so on into March ▪ the unassimilated water
frozen in the ground ▪ just waiting

▪ ▪ ▪

For the moment though ▪ this very moment ▪ the moon is setting
behind a spray of baby's breath and two stems of week-old roses on my
sill ▪ The roses will be dropping petals before the day is out ▪ but
for now neither they nor I much notice notice having been served

▪
▪

Not till dawn becomes a volunteer / Will we know
how it was inside this world;

There have to be at some points exit ramps for going down ▪
This time appoints its mercenary king inside to seize into its
prison every eye ▪ its lozenge prism ▪ my thorn boots on
the threshold ▪ Language made me in the eye of its hurricane
beholder ▪ roadlight ghosted on the calendar

▪ ▪ ▪

I don't know why I'm telling you this might translate *I know I shouldn't tell you this* into hem-haw or duck-and-cover ▪ but maybe it can lean too toward poetry as C. K. Williams spoke of it ▪ *a medium through which our attention flows* ▪ *uncolored by any necessity whatsoever*

▪ ▪ ▪

What I mean is I want to say the sayable ▪ and to say what lies
beyond the sayable ▪ What I mean is great spring clouds sail over
playgrounds ▪ kidshriek ▪ dogshout ▪ distant bells ▪ a
peal of motherlaugh ▪ shadows under carriages ▪ assorted
flags ▪ in this year before the civil war

▪
▪

language is a medium for experiencing experience.

I don't know why anyone tells anybody anything ■ but I don't think I'm
telling you this for the usual reasons whatever they are ■ I don't know
what I'm telling you when I tell you this ■ but I do know it's not
in what the words say it's in what sending them says ■ I know
the saying stands to the sending ■ as after-dark snow here stands
to pre-dawn hush

■ ■ ■

What I mean is I've seen myself from a distance but this was
different ■ What I mean is I know how you said it because I say what
you're seeing ■ I see a line of pale brown dried reeds ■ then a dark
opening in the trees ■ Perhaps you too wish to find yourself within the
sparrow ■ Perhaps you too need a lexicon of praise

■ ■ ■

What I see when I look up doesn't count but maybe should ■ the
leaf-shagged squirrel nest tiara'd with snow ■ the particular
pink the cirrus's sun-suggesting undersurface assumes only for this
moment ■ this breath-brief *now*

My eyes fill with a seeing not their own.

What I see when I look up doesn't count but maybe should ▪ the
leaf-shagged squirrel nest tiara'd with snow ▪ the particular
pink the cirrus's sun-suggesting undersurface assumes only for this
moment ▪ this breath-brief *now*

▪ ▪ ▪

I wonder is the groundhog silent in his hole ▪ or is he writing poems
with his blood and breath ▪ Are poems unaccounted for among the
ones and zeros ▪ or are they too emergent ▪ like the womb ▪ or
like the eye that so confounded Darwin

▪ ▪ ▪

I wonder why I'm telling you this ▪ instead of something else ▪
which is to wonder why certain happenings feel more meaning-rich than
others ▪ why my sending you this missive has a sense that what is sent
does not ▪ why I write these words not for their sense ▪
but so I can send them

▪ ▪ ▪

The silence grows and I can hear inside it nothing ▪ everything ▪ the
fifteen different songs of the black-capped chickadee ▪ the emphysemic
hours gasping out of days ▪ my love saying something in her low dawn
voice ▪ the barn doors sliding shut at Crescent Farm ▪ the mammal
sounds I'm terrified to name

▪

▪

what we have heard in some other life.

It's not that trucks are *loud* here more than a mile off the
highway ▪ but their not-quite-white noise does compromise the night
quiet ▪ in that ghost-trafficked hour before early risers rise ▪ so
when snow pauses those semis' otherwise persistent passing ▪ the
hush is close to perfect

▪ ▪ ▪

Mornings here a barn owl's been saying a few things about
America ▪ not insisting ▪ Juncos fat with millet and seed corn
rattle the feeders before I'm ready to wake ▪ Last year's wild cabbage
frozen in the wetlands next to Barbara and Emily's place

▪ ▪ ▪

Nothing for me to add ▪ but repetition with variation is what we
do ▪ we two and all our sibilance-thirsty siblings ▪ we soon-to-
cease-singing soon-to-be-sequestered carbon-copiers ▪ so I say
again what can't be said often enough ▪ because the futility of saying
it makes saying it urgent

▪ ▪ ▪

Some woodland beast came barking through the yard at 3 ▪ A
moonless hour ▪ I could barely see my way to pee much less identify
the thing that loosed that limbic yawp ▪ But there paused life beyond
the human ▪ Then I felt blessed because I knew one day my life would
pause ▪ (would have to pause) ▪ beyond the human too

▪

▪

we create life worlds around these wants.

It's on the list of things I'm grateful for ▪ the forked branch that in
its fall caught on a lower branch ▪ in the tree by the street ▪ and
has hung there now for years ▪ The list is long ▪ I say already
what Agnes Martin says in old age I will look back and say ▪ *I had
everything I really wanted*

▪ ▪ ▪

I want to be neither the black asphalt nor the white ice layered over
it ▪ but the silence between the layers ▪ I want to be neither the
stone fence at the foot of the neighbor's yard nor the dawnlight gathering
in the east ▪ but a particle ▪ a drowse of morning wind ▪
a wave no sense can detect ▪ eye-level and disembodied

▪ ▪ ▪

I don't want to be the hiss of tires across rain-glazed asphalt ▪ or
the swish of tires through slush ▪ but I do want to be the difference
between them in timbre ▪ and volume ▪ and pitch

▪

▪

We're dated within histories of make / in order to be made whole;

The states we pass through ▪ our words collecting traces from a
blue state here a red state there ▪ the skin fleck from a gunman in
Cheyenne ▪ the dander of a Boston abuser ▪ traces of poison rain
between a warehouse in Sheboygan and a federal mail plane

▪ ▪ ▪

Why *on* my mind and *in* my body and *underneath* it all ▪ And what
about the rain ▪ and what about our watching for it ▪ No rain as I
write this but rain forecast for later today

▪ ▪ ▪

I imagine a water cortège ▪ bearing great white blossoms through
stands of uncut catalpas ▪ toward the south and the unstopped river's
mouth ▪ high water standing among fissured trunks in the floodpan

the imaginary joins the real in a space that contains its own secret

I imagine a water cortège ▪ bearing great white blossoms through
stands of uncut catalpas ▪ toward the south and the unstopped river's
mouth ▪ high water standing among fissured trunks in the floodpan

▪ ▪ ▪

But my imagination limps more often than it gambols ▪ hears random
noises as knockings at the door ▪ I remember certain things now
more clearly than when I remembered them differently ▪ Sometimes
I ask *Didn't you hear that?* and sometimes I am asked ▪ but always the
answer is no

▪ ▪ ▪

I've been trying to imagine ▪ how this all might end ▪ My own
lone death ▪ a flashlight under sheets at night ▪ reading a comic
book ▪ I'm not sure I like

▪ ▪ ▪

Now all is owl and Love and coneshadow ▪ and steam ghosting the
meltwet shingles where the sun warms them ▪ and spindly icicles
glinting under the gutter seams ▪ than which none greater can be
conceived ▪ as syllable from sound ▪ I know not what

▪

▪

Slow moving and black lines go ceaselessly over the earth,

Now crimson light of the late American afternoon stops up the mouths of
Mahican caves in the Berkshires ▪ The Housatonic's last engine sleeps
in its nest of red nettles ▪ A band of Pittsfield militiamen shoulder
their muskets and fade into dusk ▪ until the only thing visible's a single
bandolier's metallic X

▪ ▪ ▪

They set up metal fencing all around ▪ you know the kind I mean ▪
freestanding bike-rack-like sections ▪ each eight feet long ▪ maybe
ten ▪ A shabby carnival that festers once a summer ▪
for the week they call "Jubilee Days" here in this also-shabby
outpost ▪ this loneliness refuge

▪ ▪ ▪

By which I mean ▪ to write *with* you is to write *against* you ▪ as
that aspen with the scarred limb ▪ grows *with* and leans *against* that
silver birch

▪ ▪ ▪

As having biked back from work with a re-used plastic grocery bag
dangling from the handlebars ▪ stopping in the driveway I tipped
sideways ▪ into Love's refurbished '50s camper that kept me from
falling over ▪ and made a deep drum-hollow *duhhh* ▪ when my
shoulder clumsied against it

▪

▪

looking out / at moonstruck trees

By which I mean a nightgust blew the downspout clean off the
gutter ▪ a length of alien-straight white aluminum laid out on this
morning's grass ▪ By which I mean I sometimes sink into a place
inside myself ▪ that's difficult to climb out of

▪ ▪ ▪

There's a little bit of unstained dog-eared pine fence picket
in us ▪ weather-grayed and warped away from one rail enough
to clatter out the wind's chaotic Morse ▪ There's a little bit of Phillips
head in us ▪ self-centering to tighten the two screws holding the
storm door catch tight to the jamb

▪ ▪ ▪

As thunder's gap from lightning times one's distance from a storm ▪ so
the intervals that space our conversation ▪ and our correspondence
to an ever-diminishing duration ▪ describe a fatal calculus with proofs

▪
▪

the self that you were born with turns into / The self that you created,

Yesterday's sun saved today's sun a spot just next to it
on the horizon ▪ Plenty else just like this you can't see moving but you
can see it moved ▪ If passing through particulate creates the color
of the sunset ▪ how can we know the disappearancer from
the disappearance

▪ ▪ ▪

Winter stars relinquish their positions ▪ to scatter ashes in the
grass ▪ *This* roadside barn stands upright ▪ *That* one leans ▪
I know the feeling ▪ I share with you a taste for scuffled stuff ▪
for tedium when it inclines to change the look of things ▪
if not the nature

▪ ▪ ▪

We're under some flight path here ▪ or paths ▪ It didn't take long
online to find that a great circle with SFO and JFK as points passes
directly overhead ▪ so surely that's one ▪ On my wee-hours
walkabout each morning ▪ if I can see the stars I'm certain also to
see ▪ blinking lights crossing the sky

+

like a campfire glimpsed in the distance,

We're under some flight path here ▪ or paths ▪ It didn't take long
online to find that a great circle with SFO and JFK as points passes
directly overhead ▪ so surely that's one ▪ On my wee-hours
walkabout each morning ▪ if I can see the stars I'm certain also to
see ▪ blinking lights crossing the sky

▪ ▪ ▪

What I mean is my love reads ▪ drinks coffee ▪ touches
my shoulder ▪ and a galaxy of sensations from lavender to
cherryred ▪ detonates in my solar plexus ▪ an electrobiological
burst that could make birds and planes drop from the sky

▪ ▪ ▪

There's some parable to be made of the situation ▪ about my seeing
only the lights from the plane but not the plane itself ▪ about my not
even existing for the people sleeping in their assigned seats ▪ as they
dotted-line my sky

▪ ▪ ▪

I love my love right through to her skull ▪ right through to her
fingerbones ▪ Her skull will still be her even when what is recognized
as her has worn away ▪ even when her skull has worn away leaving
only darkness ▪ even when the dark has worn away leaving only
residue ▪ even when the residue has worn away ▪ leaving only my love

▪

▪

Want-hands huming / upwards from my inwards

So much to see even at my feet ▪ the aura of damp-darkened cement
surrounding a pine cone fallen to the sidewalk ▪ and the loose irregular
hollows from snow fallen into snow around the precise circular smaller
perforations of meltdrops ▪ I am those groundsights ▪ plus the white
crust of morning gristfrost on the wooden footbridge across the creek

▪ ▪ ▪

I can see deep into the woods these months before the green swarms
back ▪ adorned with gnats and black flies ▪ Peepers weeks
early with their countless choral plosions ▪ coyote keenings in the
morning lightrise ▪ clouds torn out of larger clouds purpledark and
linenwhite ▪ On the home road glitters of shadows ▪ where the
wind gusts over a granite slab beside a storm drain

▪ ▪ ▪

Which is more silver in the sun ▪ mist risen from the river ▪ or a
million veined transparent wings hovering over it

▪ ▪ ▪

Or you ▪ who I've imagined ▪ arising in the still waters of
Oklahoma ▪ a thatch-headed boy like me ▪ Did you see the same
transparent power tensing in the woods ▪ heavy with afternoon heat
and river vapor ▪ so crammed with electric signatures of dipterans
and lepidopterans the air itself would flutter and seethe ▪ Were you
stuffed with so much green you seemed to leaf and sweat pitch ▪ so
othered you couldn't speak except to bullfrogs and wrens

▪

▪

A first unfallen / church it might have been.

The place no one who knows one knows about ▪ the place one first
disappeared *to* ▪ Mine lay under the ramshackle farmhouse my
grandparents rented when I was a kid ▪ Out a ways ▪ the road
from town more dirt than gravel ▪ all ridges and pits

▪ ▪ ▪

Closets under stairs ▪ crawlspaces and transoms ▪ secret
rooms behind brick basement walls ▪ ornamental trees whose
shrugging-down branches grew down to the ground then into the
ground ▪ refrigerator boxes ▪ under covers with a Jules Verne
novel and a flashlight ▪ up a pine tree in a stand of pines

▪ ▪ ▪

The door to my cellar was outside ▪ angled up from the dirt and out
from the house's foundation ▪ Outside light peered between the rough
doorboards but didn't enter ▪ Chill finally forced me back among the
talking-over-one-another ▪ but not until I'd metamorphosed from
unnoticed to unseen

▪
▪

we have no other interior than the world.

Each morning I happen to myself ▪ or should I say I happen
on myself ▪ seemingly self-same but how am I to tell ▪ Is
that jay wing-banging the squirrel-proof feeder the same jay as
yesterday ▪ And what about the rain ▪ Same pattern of tickings in
the downspout ▪ same thrum of finger-drummings on the roof

▪ ▪ ▪

Outdoors claims more of my head space than of my time ▪ I'm
outside only for short spans ▪ fifteen minutes twice a day to walk
to work ▪ fifteen seconds to check the mail ▪ My workspaces
all face windows so that's a lot of time spent looking out ▪ but it's
looking out from in

▪ ▪ ▪

Now the wind drops and the five-trunked pine's just *there* ▪ a cello
on a stage that's never played ▪ When I no longer have limits I will
become like the birds and the grass ▪ There's no telling *what* I might
turn into

+

More than bones, ghost- / thin skin, I'm here,

Now the wind drops and the five-trunked pine's just *there* ▪ a cello on a stage that's never played ▪ When I no longer have limits I will become like the birds and the grass ▪ There's no telling *what* I might turn into

▪ ▪ ▪

Maybe I love the racemose (delphinium, hollyhock) ▪ because I myself am cymose ▪ Maybe I've insisted to myself I'm panicled ▪ because I've known all along I'm thyrsoid

▪ ▪ ▪

I come to myself ▪ in a room in a house on a bed ▪ in another season ▪ The moon finds me ▪ and the moon's light ▪ and I'm nothing ▪ in transition

▪ ▪ ▪

I've been injured now for longer than I was healthy ▪ and partial now for longer than I was whole ▪ I've been askew now for longer than I was plumb ▪ and guilty now for longer than I was innocent ▪ I've been dying now for longer than I was living ▪ and soiled now for longer than I was clean

▪

▪

it is this visionary reality we need,

I was for use ▪ a ventriloquial device ▪ the bellows for another's
breath ▪ the plexus for another's need

▪ ▪ ▪

I can't find either ▪ where the raccoon tracks marking the morning's
new snow originate ▪ or where the love lost to lost loves and the Love
lost to the Lost Love send their fading signals from

▪ ▪ ▪

I wanted this ▪ to be the leaf-squall slumping by the undemanding
stream ▪ full of the odors of the woods at last ▪ the earth as pallid
as a frozen sheet ▪ the river cold and deep and brief

▪ ▪ ▪

Often I have perceived human bodies sound out slow steps in
the stairwell ▪ brush the gauze curtains ▪ crouch in the
fireplace ▪ creak over floorboards when the house was still ▪ and
thought they were my own ▪ and thought I was the human one

▪
▪

demented by brevity, / driven askew, evaporating.

I see the sky over the airfield ▪ towering mounds of stormtorn
dirtied burnt meringue ▪ *because* Tiepolo painted clouds that
way ▪ What I mean you will tell me or my love will tell me or the
darkness will tell me or I won't be told ▪ What I mean is death winds
a spindle of skyblue silk

▪ ▪ ▪

What I mean is the Russian olive was V-shaped ▪ like the flicker-
freckled tree in the park ▪ I mean the wet heavy snow split it at the
joint ▪ so one trunk fell toward the house ▪ and the other fell into
the street

▪ ▪ ▪

I want to be the black rim at the edge of the moonslice ▪ blacker
than the surrounding sky ▪ I want to be the cracked snowcrust
surrounding the deer tracks that cross the yard ▪ from the
nightwoods to the driveway's edge

▪
▪

But generalized magnificences cannot replace the nettle of the ravines

They don't plow here when it snows ■ and no grates sieve the sewer
drains ■ that open into the curb more than into the street itself ■ It
gives the underworld more presence ■ seeing raccoons emerge from
the drains ■ and disappear down into them

■ ■ ■

In the trash part of winter ■ having downed and traced my long
slope x describes the origin of ■ my fabergé falls in a
factory ■ rescues down whatever's left of discount crickets
the cold nights pour themselves on ■ bitter syrup ■ Best
to use the whole night to come back to oneself

■ ■ ■

It's not always November in my soul ■ but it is right now ■ I don't
wander the way I used to ■ but I wander farther the wayward way I
wander now ■ It's less wearying ■ this wanderlustless wandering

+

We must go beyond beyond to a place
where we have never been the center,

It's not always November in my soul ▪ but it is right now ▪ I don't
wander the way I used to ▪ but I wander farther the wayward way I
wander now ▪ It's less wearying ▪ this wanderlustless wandering

▪ ▪ ▪

So clever ▪ how the site of selfhood will project itself through
farthest space ▪ even in the teeth of its own dissolution ▪
especially in the teeth

▪ ▪ ▪

So tidy in their standings-ready ▪ those letters in their superpatient
arrays ▪ ABC ▪ QWERTY ▪ Tidy yet so red-alert ▪ so quick
brown fox ▪ so Horseman pass by

▪ ▪ ▪

I'm satisfied only to know that at the center of the known reposes
the unknowable ▪ the black hole at the center of the Tootsie
Pop ▪ the space ▪ unspannable ▪ between what I mean and
what I say ▪ between what I say and what you hear ▪ between
your impression of me and whatever constitutes whatever the word *I*
gestures toward

▪

▪

between always *and* to be, / *The music of hinges,*

Our lists of what we are not favor one another ▪ I am neither sense
of “replace” ▪ not replace as in *the red-shafted flicker replaces the*
yellow-shafted at the edge of its range ▪ or as in *I replaced the broken*
window pane ▪ but I breathe the breeze between them

▪ ▪ ▪

I won’t mention here the dried-blood dawns ▪ the love of
marrowbones and tresses ▪ the trestle cars coming over the grade
beside Walden Pond crammed with cotton and iron ore ▪ I won’t
mention here the unmade bed ▪ the mice inscribing teethwords on
the inside walls ▪ the opened fifth of bourbon

▪ ▪ ▪

I do say different things differently ▪ in this our I-wouldn’t-exchange-
it-for-anything exchange ▪ Am I perceiving what I have not perceived
before ▪ because I am writing to you as I have not? ▪ If it’s an
alternative genre we’ve entered into ▪ is it another world we’re in?

▪ ▪ ▪

Perhaps you too wish to migrate into the ghostfoxes stepping out of the
woodland into the darkmeadow ▪ the transmigration of the human
into the already alive ▪ Perhaps you too must find a grammar equal to
the love that overwhelms you

▪
▪

happiness and love, happiness or love.

I want to say what has to be said but is hard to say ▪ I say I keep trying
to keep trying ▪ but I have to say it's hard to do and getting harder

▪ ▪ ▪

What I mean is the ill-trained terrier at the horse farm ▪ barking
at me as I walk by ▪ What I mean is lights coming on ▪ in the old
gas fixtures

▪ ▪ ▪

What I mean is beyond my neighbors' scruffy should-have-been-
replaced-by-now shingles ▪ sundown is purpler than at this hour
yesterday ▪ same sunset as always ▪ but also a singularity I'll never
see again ▪ Call love the beauty of the one and only ▪ call this the
beauty of the one and done

▪
▪

Then there we are / side by side, looking out at the branches,

I privilege acceptance but I have my limits ▪ I love the backyard
grass because it doesn't judge ▪ the juncos at the feeder ▪
the chipmunks raiding the double suet feeder ▪ But I judge ▪
the *not-like-me* and the *never-would-I-ever* ▪ and what I fail
to accept defines me

▪ ▪ ▪

I heard you when you wrote what you wrote ▪ and I hear you when
you write what you write ▪ I say it's not nothing to be of a mind not to
never-mind ▪ and it's sure not nothing to be of one mind

▪ ▪ ▪

What if we watched the same movie ▪ what if we told the same
joke ▪ On one specific day in these unspooling days I will hold only
darkness in my arms ▪ and then I will hold only nothing ▪ and then
only nothing will be holding me

+

nothing of north / unknown, as the dark / comes earlier.

What if we watched the same movie ▪ what if we told the same joke ▪ On one specific day in these unspooling days I will hold only darkness in my arms ▪ and then I will hold only nothing ▪ and then only nothing will be holding me

▪ ▪ ▪

Nothing 'gainst Time's scythe can make defense ▪ Nothing can bring back the hour of splendor in the grass and glory in the flower ▪ Nothing gold can stay ▪ Nothing is sturdy nothing is majestic

▪ ▪ ▪

Nothing goes into anything an infinity of times ▪ Everything has an infinity of nothing in it ▪ Plus is a change agent ▪ Times is not

▪ ▪ ▪

It's one thing to *enter* a structure something other inhabits ▪ another to *stay* ▪ At first the haunting cries at night do come from out there ▪ all far-off windborne animal wailings ▪ leaving in here safe ▪ the furnishings inanimate the fixtures unvoiced ▪ but not for long if you listen

▪

▪

When I speak now I discern a new frequency / and different others listen.

Into the long lipless mouth of the large blue postbox I place your
letter ▪ I place the postbox in a wood and grow moss overtop
of it ▪ Your letter lies all night in the empty metal belly of the
postbox ▪ For it the dark cavern ▪ the late night air ▪ the
nothing-to-do-but-wait

▪ ▪ ▪

Others text but let us presence ▪ I level with you as fully
as I can ▪ as much as I level with anybody ▪ weighting my words
with your way-with words ▪ I say what I didn't know I didn't know
how to say

▪ ▪ ▪

I say ascending into the sky's not bad ▪ the land's edge and then the
ocean's ▪ I say seen from afar ▪ I say seen from above

▪ ▪ ▪

I say for lakes out here ▪ this sky-dry high desert tenders
only shallow seasonals of irrigation runoff ▪ fringed white
with 6-12-12 ▪ congealed by algal bloom ▪ host to no
scaup ▪ home to no smallmouth

▪
▪

being addressed constitutes us as subjects from the very beginning.

I say the dark spots on the backs of my hands become invisible at
distance ▪ I say I carry the record of all my abrasions within me

▪ ▪ ▪

I keep seeing a nest in the notch ▪ where I know it's just a knob ▪ I
have said the words *a good death* out loud to someone ▪ with a
straight face

▪ ▪ ▪

Humantalk ▪ birdsong ▪ humansong ▪ birdtalk ▪ People
say *I dunno but maybe* ▪ People say *no but I* do *know* ▪ People say
everybody's gonna be fat and happy

▪

▪

Don't you know this is a poem about longing?

Out here occasional cabins pimple the hills ▪ but it's mostly BLM land
and Union Pacific right-of-way and national forest ▪ "Multi-use" is the
going term for *ATVs bring in more revenue than ruby-crowned kinglets*
do ▪ "Decibelspill" is my word for how much farther ▪ the sputter
and rasp of a snowmobile carries through crisp air ▪ than in foraging
a solitaire ranges

▪ ▪ ▪

I once thought words would come to me following sight ▪ the way
these turkey poults follow their hen ▪ unsteady but sure along the
road's edge ▪ then almost stately in the weedgrowth ▪ their
element ▪ which is a kind of poetry

▪ ▪ ▪

No words for the wordlessness that is not nothing ▪ No words that *do*
name What Has No Name ▪ No words that *don't* ▪ No words not
interstitial intermezzic interoperate ▪ No word but makes something
of nothing

+

my self-consciousness is not only suspended, but temporarily abolished

No words for the wordlessness that is not nothing ▪ No words that *do* name What Has No Name ▪ No words that *don't* ▪ No words not interstitial intermezzic interoperate ▪ No word but makes something of nothing

▪ ▪ ▪

Your silence my darkness ▪ your darkness my words ▪ your words my silence

▪ ▪ ▪

No word does *not* take years to read ▪ in the poem that is a poem ▪ No words anywhere ▪ other than between the paint and the wall ▪ for the Nothing to Be Done About It

▪ ▪ ▪

If I were made in the image of any god she would have to be a god of erasure ▪ but I keep writing into absence ▪ hoping to preserve some trace

▪
▪

the farthest outpost of solitude nothing can touch,

There's one chair I spend a lot of time in ■ laptop open ■ lap desk
resting on the chair's hardwood arms ■ facing a window that looks out
on the intersection ■ of a through street and a cross street
with stop signs

■ ■ ■

I wish for mist and star-sparkle ■ and a long vista over which my
paper cylinder unravels like a spent firework ■ but I don't know and
no one knows how all this is going to end

■ ■ ■

It's been given me often by others ■ Julian's assurance that all shall be
well ■ so I *want* to believe it ■ and I've given it often to others *as if*
I believed it ■ but in fact I don't

■ ■ ■

I return most days to the place where two trails diverge in the town
forest ■ the white trail right-angling from the blue ■ There's the
trail map in its *Boys' Life*–style hutch ■ there's the downed pine that
a town arborist must've sectioned decades ago ■ there's the low
stretch of swamp that dries up by June ■ but this morning brims with
snowmelt and leafrot

■
■

Your mind / like a pilot light inside your sleep,

It's noisier than you'd think in the middle of the night in the middle of
nowhere ▪ This town is small and not near any other ▪ but from
my house in one direction it's not a mile to the interstate ▪ and in
another direction it's only a few blocks to the railroad yard ▪ so there's
noise at all hours

▪ ▪ ▪

Something happens in the hills at night ▪ the otherworldly
howling ▪ the hollowed hollows ▪ What sounds like lament is
really praise

▪ ▪ ▪

Wait for me is a different *wait* than *wait and see* ▪ He hath ever
but tenderly known himself ▪ Doesn't matter that it lasts only
seconds ▪ elbows on my desk ▪ each cheekbone in one cupped
palm ▪ it's still sleep

▪
▪

none / of the words I hold would salve and lily

What I mean is passengers Hikes Hook and Blue please proceed to Gate D29 ▪ What I mean is please board at this time

▪ ▪ ▪

What I mean is they're not facing each other ▪ they're both looking in the same direction ▪ out of the frame to the viewer's left

▪ ▪ ▪

I mean a motorbike's whine receding down Pine like a chased
fly ▪ your letter of blessings creased but clear ▪ last night cool
enough to kill the central air ▪ and raise the bedroom windows

+

to be in a landscape / where purity isn't possible

I mean a motorbike's whine receding down Pine like a chased
fly ▪ your letter of blessings creased but clear ▪ last night cool
enough to kill the central air ▪ and raise the bedroom windows

▪ ▪ ▪

Sounds like the downy I heard yesterday repeating its one-note
song ▪ Who knew woodpeckers *sang*? ▪ Can one note be a
song? ▪ Not quite the music of the spheres ▪ that red-naped
monoglot's monotone gotta-be-me ▪ but I've heard worse

▪ ▪ ▪

I turned the tap and out came a stream of bees ▪ I got married
to ash on the threshold of a ziggurat ▪ I climbed imaginary
switchbacks with a switchblade in my belt ▪ I washed my face
with spindrift from the sky

▪ ▪ ▪

Water has no taste or smell or color ▪ water itself I mean the pure
substance ▪ that never occurs in its pure state ▪ In these sparse
desert sloughs though ▪ it asserts that burn-your-nostrils yellow-
green ▪ instead of assuming at sundown the cool of ancient made-by-
someone-long-since-nameless celadon

▪

▪

Concentrations of impurity serially interrupt and entangle one another.

There's nothing pure or even half-clean in these post-pandemic years ▪ these pre-what years ▪ the state is sick with its own history ▪ The duck chicks hatched sick in the chicken hutch and died

▪ ▪ ▪

The Swainson's settled with its kill atop the twelve-foot-square industrial HVAC unit ▪ and didn't startle ▪ didn't stop eviscerating that squirrel ▪ when the compressor blasted on

▪ ▪ ▪

If the perfect were the pure ▪ then any quality would be a falling off ▪ so the truly pure could only be the unmanifest

▪ ▪ ▪

For all I *had* seen at this intersection ▪ schoolkids on bikes pedaling right through the stop sign without looking ▪ cars running the stop sign ▪ an oblivious toddler in the middle of the through street with no parent or sitter in sight ▪ a dumbass neighbor doing wheelies on his crotch rocket ▪ it's amazing I *hadn't* seen a wreck

▪

▪

treetops so distant / they register at first as smoke.

A strong hold happens later ▪ Refugee sun declines behind a wall of trees ▪ A floating multifocal eye

▪ ▪ ▪

What mediates between at my feet and overhead ▪ might be matter and measure ▪ I've learned from Love to watch for shitpiles under trees ▪ as cues to where owls might be hiding in the crown ▪ I never would have guessed that this would occupy me ▪ would be me

▪ ▪ ▪

But there I go again ▪ pouring from the emptiness inside into that other emptiness ▪ defining *torus* ▪ or rather it's my best attempt ▪ at fathoming a world without me

▪
▪

between oneself and the thing all the vertical, the refusal, of height.

As measured with coffee spoons and steeples swimming in amethyst and o'erbrimming of bees' clammy cells ▪ I am almost out of time ▪ If I could emulate the Deep Space Climate Observatory ▪ sending back images of earth from beyond its gravitational field ▪ I would be out of time

▪ ▪ ▪

Perhaps you too must every day begin again as if from scratch ▪ this given day ▪ exceeding you by every measure ▪ Perhaps you too want to go on the death adventure ▪ Perhaps you too want to pass through the final door

▪ ▪ ▪

No lie ▪ No exaggeration ▪ No word left behind ▪ No irritable reaching after fact or reason ▪ To learn ▪ To listen ▪ To learn to listen

+

Your whole age sits between what you hear / and what you write

No lie ▪ No exaggeration ▪ No word left behind ▪
No irritable reaching after fact or reason ▪ To learn ▪
To listen ▪ To learn to listen

▪ ▪ ▪

To the universe the diverging subjects of my personhood haltingly advance ▪ I have written myself to all ▪ who must get what the writing means ▪ Away! Away! ▪ for I will fly to thee

▪ ▪ ▪

Hard to think what any of us could say to any other ▪ other than what in your letter you say to me ▪ and what here I say back to you ▪ Its being all anyone can say ▪ makes the saying feel urgent

▪ ▪ ▪

People say *I don't have the patience for that* ▪ People say *don't get me wrong* ▪ People say *emergencies are usually not too often*

▪
▪

or call / into a well where someone has fallen in.

People say *time travel* and *time trouble* and *timeout* and *overtime* ▪ People say *tell me about it* ▪ People say *don't got* and *him and his cousin* ▪ People say *another time*

▪ ▪ ▪

I speak *because of* not *in spite of* silence ▪ as I move toward the door at the end of the dark corridor ▪ I speak to one but hope the many hear ▪ I want to know that I've been heard

▪ ▪ ▪

I hear what you're saying because I see how you said it ▪ These fragments I have sheared off from my ruins ▪ for serial rather than sum ▪ string rather than heap ▪ popcorn threaded to trim the tree not in inevitable sequence ▪ this kernel by necessity first ▪ but not in random sequence either

▪ ▪ ▪

What I mean is ▪ listening is all

▪

▪

The fragment as spoken by the one lost His heart singing in its dish

Into the otherwise clean library book ▪ some previous borrower has taped a small slip of ruled paper ▪ the coarse school-tablet kind ▪ on which in ballpoint is handwritten ▪ *I asked the generals if this is how we fight wars. They both said, "This is worse than war! We're killing our own!"*

▪ ▪ ▪

What of all those poems that have fallen away ▪ do they change the air ▪ do they change the composition of one's life ▪ and if they do what kind of change ▪ chemical electrical or nuclear

▪ ▪ ▪

What of one poet who ▪ in the middle of one life's journey from just lost to long lost ▪ woke well and truly lost ▪ not lost to longing ▪ but not long for this wait-and-see

▪

▪

She broods on clouds, / hears voices in wind.

Soft wind snakes among dried stalks ▪ that click and hiss beside a
shuttered DIY store ▪ Everywhere a door or barrier ▪ as though
the only way to go were *through*

▪ ▪ ▪

At some point it stopped making sense to *speak* when I knelt ▪ If I can't
believe anything I say I can't believe myself ▪ I don't petition because
what for and to whom ▪ I do stay on my knees because how else

▪ ▪ ▪

Not absence of meaning but *other* meaning ▪ Not absence of value
but *other* value ▪ A poetry of plain stripped language ▪ free of
noise and poison

+

the negative where all identity is lost,

Not absence of meaning but *other* meaning ▪ Not absence of value
but *other* value ▪ A poetry of plain stripped language ▪ free of
noise and poison

▪ ▪ ▪

Not the two T-boned cars ▪ one still in the intersection ▪ one
right-angled to the curb facing a stranger's sidewalk ▪ but the two
scruffy dudes from the one car ▪ furious at the skinny girl from the
other ▪ Not the wreck itself ▪ but the aftermath

▪ ▪ ▪

I'm not expecting any answer ▪ but I do speak often into
darkness ▪ Those thistles would be yellow ▪ if the moonlight
brightened by a hundred lux

▪ ▪ ▪

No words that do what they say ▪ No words that don't dis-ease ▪
Nor I nor any man that but man is ▪ with nothing shall be
pleased ▪ till he be eased ▪ with being nothing

▪
▪

And then there was the nothing that was something else,

Are photons from the moon's light different from table-lamp
photons ■ having traveled through space ■ I want to be the pale
blue light inside the road ice ■ the distance separating the satellites

■ ■ ■

Not the strike ■ what I see of the owl ■ but what was
struck ■ the now decapitated pigeon ■ that must have
been suddenly taloned from its roost ■ winged to the nearby
spruce ■ and beaked in two ■ all within seconds

■ ■ ■

These questions no one has answered ■ so we're forced to proceed
by way of undefined terms ■ as if we could understand one
another ■ If I'm made in the image of any god she would have to be a
god of errors ■ or else there's nothing of me there to recognize

■ ■ ■

The morning after the first headless pigeon ■ a second lay at the base
of the same tree ■ The next morning nothing ■ but that doesn't
mean when the sun rises this morning ■ there won't be a fresh corpse

■

■

true existence is in the Abyss. Yes, *trusted to night and silence.*

Along the woods path shine the nighteyes ▪ and over the fields lines of fences ▪ going all along the way into the distance and up into the hills ▪ and above the hills the murmurations

▪ ▪ ▪

New tracks every morning in old snow show how much happens without my seeing it ▪ My yard's bad that way ▪ and my head's worse

▪ ▪ ▪

Now zoom way out ▪ or zoom way in ▪ It's all fields of probability and minuscule remainders ▪ ones replacing zeros ▪ zeros negating ones ▪ the violence of the binary ▪ At zero Kelvin all particle activity ceases and "all disorder disappears" ▪ I know of no other rest

I want everyone here to survive what is coming.

I don't cry at funerals ▪ don't cry at all ▪ I'm not the age I'd hope
for if I were pulling numbers from a hat ▪ and I'm not living where I
ever thought I would ▪ but you should see the sky here ▪ its daily
omigodnesses of color and change

▪ ▪ ▪

And you should hear the leaves here ▪ heart-shaped and
serrate ▪ oak-profiled maple classic alternate opposite spiral
whorled ▪ their sound like rain but antecedent to rain ▪ like ocean
but antecedent to ocean ▪ a call to which the rain responds

▪ ▪ ▪

You should see the squirrels and sparrows here ▪ moonscaping with
their dustbaths what would be lawn if I watered ▪ I know it's just to
diminish discomfort and protest parasites ▪ but it still looks *gotta boogie*
to me ▪ still looks plenty Charleston ▪ Charo ▪ Cha Cha Cha

+

clouds parting, // low rumble of thunder, then / light

You should see the squirrels and sparrows here ▪ moonscaping with
their dustbaths what would be lawn if I watered ▪ I know it's just to
diminish discomfort and protest parasites ▪ but it still looks *gotta boogie*
to me ▪ still looks plenty Charleston ▪ Charo ▪ Cha Cha Cha

▪ ▪ ▪

Remember when the August rain would dash the bedroom
windows ▪ hard summer rain ▪ and the sun would hide behind a
scrim all day ▪ prefiguring October ▪ a proof to prevent happiness
from fading

▪ ▪ ▪

Remember the edgeworn earthtone braided oval rug ▪ securing the
dustlit living room ▪ and the shovel and hoe ▪ rusting in the clay-
cold cellar under it

▪ ▪ ▪

What I mean is the windows of the world were painted silver ▪ the
feeling of growing into myself and away from the world ▪ the feeling of
time without verbs ▪ space without subjects ▪ the onflowingness
of what flows from force to force and fern to fern

▪
▪

In other words, there is no poem of one's own,

Here are the rusting dumpsters that running-stitch the alleys ■ in
the dilapidated downtown ■ Here are the RVs that tack the Walmart
parking lot ■ to the sweep of scrub that stretches away from the
off-ramp

■ ■ ■

Here are the driveway divots where the asphalt's fallen in ■ the
sinkholes that brim with rain

■ ■ ■

Here are my double-shelved books ■ the spines of the ones upright in
the back row obscured ■ by their perpendiculars ■ the horizontal
ones in half-height stacks in front

■ ■ ■

Here is the mill with the humming of thunder ■ Here is the body stood
apart from the soul ■ Here is the fragile soap-bubble skin ■ the
thin glass of seeing

■
■

The seamless transfer of two people / humming

If the urge for belonging is universal and ultimate ▪ if everyone wants
more than anything else to belong ▪ then where does that leave
me ▪ who wants intimacy more

▪ ▪ ▪

I think the self might be an envelope inside a fire ▪ Its stuff goes up in
thin black streams ▪ enlarging the sky

▪ ▪ ▪

Or Mrs. Foote wheeling in a spinet ▪ and sweeping a musical staff
onto the fifth-grade classroom board with a five-stick
chalkholder ▪ Every good boy did fine but I got lost along the
way ▪ drifted dimwittedly from fan base to absentee ballot ▪
from orchestra seating to first-round bye

▪
▪

remarks on the barely perceptible disappearances from our world

The house sparrow cadging muffin crumbs beneath the café's
outdoor tables has something of me in him ▪ and I have something
of him in me

▪ ▪ ▪

What should I do now in these clearings where I don't
belong ▪ but where else end ▪ what exists to merge with and
continue ▪ something larger than itself

▪ ▪ ▪

The whole reveals itself immediately before its dissolution ▪ In the
beginning were the letters ▪ In the end ▪ the ashes of my fire-
cleaned sheets

+

Things look different when we do not / defend ourselves from them.

Send word to eyedropper-feed our birdmouth urge ■ to listen
to rain-glossolalic downspouts and look at rain-lensed driveway
divots ■ our urge to watch for echoes and listen for reflections ■
of the Unmeasured Measurer

■ ■ ■

I remember the last time I felt this way ■ I brought metal in a
box ■ a half head of deer ■ cloven ■ clovered ■ clove of
bone ■ that savory radius ■ my cells fill with liquids not their own

■ ■ ■

What I see when I look up doesn't count but maybe should ■ the
leaf-shagged squirrel nest tiara'd with snow ■ the particular
pink the cirrus's sun-suggesting undersurface assumes only for this
moment ■ this breath-brief *now*

■ ■ ■

I imagine a water cortège ■ bearing great white blossoms through
stands of uncut catalpas ■ toward the south and the unstopped river's
mouth ■ high water standing among fissured trunks in the floodpan

■
■

together, / without meaning to, without meaning anything, / we sang

We're under some flight path here ▪ or paths ▪ It didn't take long
online to find that a great circle with SFO and JFK as points passes
directly overhead ▪ so surely that's one ▪ On my wee-hours
walkabout each morning ▪ if I can see the stars I'm certain also to
see ▪ blinking lights crossing the sky

▪ ▪ ▪

Now the wind drops and the five-trunked pine's just *there* ▪ a cello
on a stage that's never played ▪ When I no longer have limits I will
become like the birds and the grass ▪ There's no telling *what* I might
turn into

▪ ▪ ▪

It's not always November in my soul ▪ but it is right now ▪ I don't
wander the way I used to ▪ but I wander farther the wayward way I
wander now ▪ It's less wearying ▪ this wanderlustless wandering

▪ ▪ ▪

What if we watched the same movie ▪ what if we told the same
joke ▪ On one specific day in these unspooling days I will hold only
darkness in my arms ▪ and then I will hold only nothing ▪ and then
only nothing will be holding me

▪
▪

And the memory of the dust vanished immediately.

No words for the wordlessness that is not nothing ▪ No words that *do*
name What Has No Name ▪ No words that *don't* ▪ No words not
interstitial intermezzic interoperate ▪ No word but makes something
of nothing

▪ ▪ ▪

I mean a motorbike's whine receding down Pine like a chased
fly ▪ your letter of blessings creased but clear ▪ last night cool
enough to kill the central air ▪ and raise my bedroom windows

▪ ▪ ▪

No lie ▪ No exaggeration ▪ No word left behind ▪
No irritable reaching after fact or reason ▪ To learn ▪
To listen ▪ To learn to listen

▪
▪

We need not fear these   silences, —

Not absence of meaning but *other* meaning ▪ Not absence of value
but *other* value ▪ A poetry of plain stripped language ▪ free of
noise and poison

▪ ▪ ▪

You should see the squirrels and sparrows here ▪ moonscaping with their
dustbaths what would be lawn if I watered ▪ I know it's just to diminish
discomfort and protest parasites ▪ but it still looks *gotta boogie* to
me ▪ still looks plenty Charleston ▪ Charo ▪ Cha Cha Cha

▪ ▪ ▪

The whole reveals itself immediately before its dissolution ▪ In the
beginning were the letters ▪ In the end ▪ the ashes of my fire-
cleaned sheets

(each. other.)

THE MOMENTS OF POETIC LANGUAGE that nimbus our exchange all are the words of others – poets, essayists, novelists, theorists, inspirations, teachers, friends, crushes, loves, exes. This chorus sifts its voices over us as stars sift their light on a clear night.

Having embraced their words as blessings, we here declare our gratitude in the form of blessings, wishes, promises, and impossible exchanges.

To **Barbara Guest**, from whose *Forces of Imagination* we have borrowed "**The poem begins**...," we deed a quiet stretch of beach animated by a chilly spring wind, to wander at her leisure, by herself or with whom she pleases, gathering "driftwood of the unconscious."

For **Paul Celan**, whose "You may" begins "You may confidently...," we're hard at work inventing a new language, one never before spoken, with three hundred new words for *darkness* and six hundred new words for *light*.

To **Elizabeth Bishop**, who records the moment "I looked into his eyes..." in "The Fish," we give a pair of finding glasses, made with lenses of old scratched isinglass.

On **Will Alexander**, whose words "I ascribe to you combustive..." come from his poem "Combustion & Leakage," we bestow a gilded, mirrored crown etched with the countless spirits of *vodún*.

+

To you, **Fernando Pessoa**, from whose *The Book of Disquiet* we have taken the sentence "**There was never this hour**...," we deliver the key to a dim, elegantly appointed ground-floor flat on Lisbon's Avenida de Liberdade, opposite Palácio Foz. The back door lets out onto a private meadow filled with all of your memories, including the ones you can't remember.

Of **William Blake**, who included "Damn. braces..." among his "Proverbs of Hell," and who needs nothing from us, we merely affirm his having what he already has, Worlds of Eternity in which he shall live forever.

For **Claire Wahmanholm**, in whose "Parallax" appears "My body and this field...," we invent an ice mountain that will not melt, and in that mountain we place a cave, and in the wall of that cave we place a window – an amber fox's eye that will not blink.

What shall we say to **Gwendolyn Brooks**, who in her poem "the mother" wonders "oh, what shall I say...," if not that we say ourselves fortunate to overhear her words, and we see waving over them, and over her, a gold-flecked beautiful banner.

+

Like **Joyelle McSweeney**, we too are waiting for "**someone to shout instructions from the sky**," as she writes in "8.14.20: River Phoenix," or even from the earth. Until that time, let her words, and these of ours, constitute our strange meeting.

In thanks to **Adrienne Rich**, from whose "At a Bach Concert" come the four words "proud restraining purity / Restores," we return *her* gift: not one thing or even a system, but an increasing complexity.

In her poem "Study of Air in Triangles," **Brenda Hillman** gives us the line "Not till dawn becomes a volunteer..." We give her, in return, six bottles of smoke. When inhaled, Bottles 1 through 5 confer the ability to render the language of the five elements into poetry. Bottle 6, when opened in a government facility, translates doublespeak into birdsong.

Lyn Hejinian in *The Language of Inquiry* alerts us that "language is a medium...," and to her we report (like children reporting to a doting parent, sure the parent will share their excitement) that both of us think we see things fluttering in and out of narration.

+

To **James Merrill**, who wrote "**My eyes fill** ..." in his poem "Walking All Night," we extend an invitation to an intimate soirée in the Byzantine Church of the Panagias, in Agia Triada. Countess Báthory has already accepted, so RSVP at your earliest. We will contact you shortly via Ouija board.

We give **Virginia Woolf**, whose essay "The Perfect Language" includes "what we have heard...," not the fish itself that has found the end of a line that hangs down into the sea but the thrill and quiver of the line at which the fish tugs.

To **Sara Ahmed**, whose words "we create life worlds..." come from *The Promise of Happiness*, we turn over our happiness scripts, not thinking she gains from the gift, but more the way two schoolkids would forfeit to their teacher the note they've been caught passing back and forth in class.

We can't think of anything to give **Ed Roberson**, from whose poem "Topoi" we mooched the line "We're dated within histories of make...," more valuable than the floating multifocal eye his books have given us. Let these words be a start, at least, at some form of recompense.

+

In thanks, **Anne Dufourmantelle**, for your loan of "**the imaginary joins**..." from *Power of Gentleness*, we'll be giving you a person, a stone, a thought, a gesture, and a color. We haven't settled yet on the first four, but the color comes from the back of a golden-olive woodpecker, against a mossed trunk in the shade of thick leafcover.

Dear **Walt Whitman**, thank you for your "Slow moving and black lines..." and the poem "To Think of Time" from which it comes. We too loafe and invite your soul; we too lean and loafe and observe, in a spear of summer grass, your large and multitudinous self.

Of course we keep the gifts themselves that **Robert Hayden** gives, such as the view the speaker in his poem "Ice Storm" sees "looking out / at moonstruck trees," but we give back in gratitude the gift that makes those gifts gifts: pattern at once wild and free.

To **John Koethe**, who included "the self that you were born with turns into..." in his poem "A Private Singularity," we proffer the precise moment when the Wisconsin sun, setting over a flooded cranberry bog, turns the entire landscape marigold and rose.

+

We give you a golden bird, **Kate Northrop**, not because we've borrowed "**like a campfire glimpsed**..." from your poem "My Mother's Outside," but because one of us is in love with you. It's not a hammered-gold mechanical bird, but a feathered breath-warm yellow warbler, and it sings not to lords and ladies but in high clear notes to you in your dreams.

PJ Harvey's "Want-hands huming...." appear in her poem "Things I Found in Gore Woods: November 26th." We offer her the sound of the wind passing through the branches in those woods, and the spotlight of the winter sun.

For the "first unfallen / church..." we've been following since we read "Song of the Andoumboulou: 60," we dedicate the Great Light behind the sky on page 23 to **Nathaniel Mackey**.

Paul Chan, thank you for the loan of "we have no other interior..." from your *Selected Writings 2000–2014*. Neither of us is authorized to act on behalf of SAIC, but so what: We here officially forgive your student loans. We say, not thinking it exerts influence but wanting it to convey respect: Keep making in freedom the work you are making in the service of freedom.

+

If we could arrange it, we'd give **Martha Collins**, whose "**More than bones, ghost-**..." we cadged from her poem "Over Time," the power to be us for one night, so that she could experience first-hand how delightful it is to spend time in her company.

We're grateful, **Anni Albers**, to your *Selected Writings on Design* for the declaration that "it is this visionary reality we need." There's this sheep farm in England that one of us has visited, where they do everything by hand and with traditional methods, from the raising of their Wensleydales through the spinning of their yarn. We give you, for whom "material is a means of communication," transportation there at will.

To **Charles O. Hartman**, whose "demented by brevity..." appears in the poem "A Glorious Sky," we gift Django Reinhardt's right hand, Wes Montgomery's left hand, James Wright's elegance circa 1960, and the Art Ensemble of Chicago's nerve circa 1970, to be used however he wishes until the end of the world.

Of course we'll need his permission to stay, but we've applied for visas to the world **Édouard Glissant**, whose *Poetic Intention* includes "But generalized magnificences...," has envisioned, in which there is neither center nor periphery.

+

For **Natalie Diaz**, from whom we borrowed the line "**We must go beyond beyond**..." from her poem "The First Water Is the Body," we have invented *Diazarin*, a shade of blue so black you can see stars inside it.

Into the care of **Eric Pankey**, whose "Clarity" contains the lines beginning "between *always*...," we entrust a reliquary that is, let's just say, "on permanent loan" from a museum that won't notice it's missing. It does contain the distal phalange from the left thumb of a saint, though we don't know *which* saint. The relics it holds that we *can* identify are not objects but essences: of cinder, anise, and noon's tin-edge heat.

To **Hélène Cixous**, from whose *Readings* comes the passage "happiness and love...," we tender one river crossing, in a creaking wooden boat rowed by a disquieting stranger.

Is it too simplistic, or unrealistic, to wish that the happiness expressed in the line "Then there we are..." in her poem "The New Winter" should pervade every moment of **Amy M. Clark**'s life? No – we think it's a fair exchange: the poem written for the life lived.

+

Josephine Jacobsen, we have borrowed from "It Is the Season" your words "**nothing of north**...," but our thanks is for your whole body of poetry, not only those lines. *As* thanks, we address *to* you these words we learned *from* you, and always say aloud into the air when we read your work: Here is water.

For writing the poem "Winterberries" and its line "When I speak now...," but not only for that, **Kevin McLellan** deserves to become fully and finally himself, and to be fully and finally *seen*.

To **Annika Thiem**, whose *Unbecoming Subjects* includes the passage beginning "being addressed...," we give two tin cans connected by a long string. We're sure she'll recycle them (not a very useful gift, we know), but we also hope that first she'll put one of the cans up to an ear, because into the other we've declared our recognition that we are addressed by her even without having met her, and *were* addressed by her even before having read her words.

For **Kevin Prufer**, who put "Don't you know..." in his "Mechanical Bird," we conjure a long gray afternoon at a billiard table in a deserted pool hall in Euclid, a pack of Marlboro Lights, a never-ending pint of bottom-fermented

Hofbräu Winterzwickl, and afterward a midnight stroll through a field of untracked snow.

+

Simple declaration of thanks seemed to us inadequate, **Lisa Robertson**, so in response to your *Nilling*, from which we've cited "**my self-consciousness is**...," we join in the exchange of vulnerabilities it initiates.

You taught us everything we know about linking and shifting, **Debra Kang Dean**. We trust you won't mind us commandeering your line "the farthest outpost..." from "World Enough" for our own purposes here. Let's plan to meet again someday in Thoreau's bean-field – *if* we can find it.

Wayne Miller! We imagine an alternate timeline in which we all live in the same town, or at least the same part of the country. But for now, we take solace in your presence via "Your mind / like a pilot light..." from your poem "Mind-Body Problem."

To **Dante Di Stefano**, from whose poem "Reading Gwendolyn Brooks to Tenth Graders" we borrow "none / of the words...," we give a notebook with a unicorn on the front cover. We don't care if you tear out the pages at the perforations or leave the fringe, we just like the miracles you perform in that purple, bubble-letter block print.

+

We appreciate the line "**to be in a landscape**...," from your spectacular "Headlands Quadrats," **Brian Teare**. We observe your multitudinous self, too, in Whitman's spear of summer grass.

We doubt we have anything to give **Fred Moten** that he would actually want, so in thanks for the "Concentrations of impurity..." on loan from *Black and Blur* we promise to keep at the task he's assigned us until it manifests as multiple solitude in fictional splice.

Were we lords of space and time, we'd give **Steven Cramer** the 1980s back, and even the 1970s, if he wanted them, and we'd restore to ourselves the moment when we first read "treetops so distant..." in the poem "Lack," so that we could experience afresh the frisson of *seeing* through his wise, and wised-up, eyes.

Marina Tsvetaeva, your phrase "between oneself and the thing..." is the least of our borrowings from *Art in the Light of Conscience*. So far, our lungs have not sufficed, but we keep trying to breathe its air.

+

How better to honor **W. S. Merwin**, whose line "**Your whole age**..." comes to us via the poem "Sibyl," than simply (simply) to stop and to listen.

To **Michelle Boisseau**, whose poem "The Anatomy Theater at Padua" contains the passage "or call / into a well...," we give – never mind that it's only a giving *back* – a million million pleasing weirdnesses, starting with an oversized church pew, big enough that an adult (ignoring the boring eulogy or sermon) can press her belly against the seat edge and swing her legs.

To **Renée Ashley**, whose "[how to put it]" opens with "The fragment as spoken...," we give a necklace strung with beads of salt-worn glass, not thinking she would ever wear it, but because of one of its glass chips: If you hold it up to the light just right, you don't merely *hear* the sea, you *become* it.

We're not sure if **Joyce Peseroff** wants to go back to 1978, but at least one of us does – to haunt her undergraduate workshop, like the Ghost of Poetry Future. Meanwhile, we're grateful for the line "She broods on clouds..." and the poem "A Revelation" from whence it comes.

+

What to give the one whose essay "The Death of the Author" gave us the phrase "**the negative where all**..."? After reflection the choice seemed inevitable, and we think you'll like it, **Roland Barthes**: We assign you the *I declare* of kings and the *I sing* of the ancient poets.

Following Wisława Szymborska's dictum "Nothing's a gift, it's all on loan," we thank you, **Teresa Cader**, for advancing us "And then there was the nothing..." from your poem "The New Creation." We hope that our use of it here pays you back, with interest.

On the left arm of **Susan Howe**, from whose *My Emily Dickinson* the words "true existence..." derive, we imprint a strangely translucent birthmark in the shape of a ladder. Only for a day, and of course it's not *really* there, but it does lead to an outside state outside of States.

We too want everyone here to survive what is coming, **Barry Lopez**, as you wrote in *Horizon*. So many ironies. Still, we carry your feathers, and your inimitable sentences, to the edge of the language, beyond which can be discerned the first glisterings of what you've called "the imagination that gives shape to the universe."

+

To **Nathan McClain**, whose phrase "**clouds parting**..." appears in the poem "Where the View Was Clearer," we convey two thousand acres of pristine Berkshire woodlands, even if only in our imaginations, where the sun goes down but never sets.

José Lezama Lima, in return for our having lifted from *A Poetic Order of Excess* your asseveration that "there is no poem of one's own," we give you this: in your own sleep to embrace a sleeping dance in the grips of a nightmare.

"To Assemble This Poem Properly," we wish for **Derek Mong** a page that keeps extending endlessly to the right as he keeps pushing his probing, inquiring lines in that direction, into the silence the blank part of the page represents. Let his words and our wish perform "The seamless transfer..." of which he writes.

To **C. D. Wright**, from whose *Cooling Time* we took "remarks on the barely...," we give back the mason jars we've been borrowing, each refilled with what it contained: one with mud, one with butter, one with barbecue sauce.

Not only for "**Things look different**...," which comes from her *Bird on a Window Sill*, but for all her work (of writing and of literary citizenship) we thank **Katerina Stoykova**. We send her a bird house in which a certain warbler will nest, from which two little feathers have gotten stuck, one feather in a shirt belonging to one of us, one in a shirt belonging to the other. This warbler occasionally will attempt to grasp the pane of Katerina's window, but we know she'll understand.

Hey, man. We've borrowed "together, / without meaning..." from your *Ornaments*, **David Daniel**, and we haven't settled yet on what to give as thanks (Juan Rulfo isn't returning our calls), so for now we're just following you in wonder, looking you in the eye and blessing you.

The novel *Amulet*, by **Roberto Bolaño**, gave us the sentence beginning "And the memory..." Upon the author we hereby confer, in perpetuity, the Poet Laureateship of the Obliterated Future.

To **John Cage**, from whose *Silence* we derived "We need not fear...," we offer